Lerner SPORTS

SPORTS
ALL-ST★RS

SUNI
LEE

Jon M. Fishman

Lerner Publications ◆ Minneapolis

SPORTS THRILLS *MEET* RESEARCH SKILLS

Lerner SPORTS

Free Database Trial: **lernersports.com**

Lerner Publications Company
An imprint of Lerner Publishing Group, Inc.
241 First Avenue North
Minneapolis, MN 55401 USA

For reading levels and more information, look up this title at www.lernerbooks.com.

Main body text set in Albany Std. Typeface provided by Agfa.

Editor: Lauren Foley

Library of Congress Cataloging-in-Publication Data

The Cataloging-in-Publication Data for *Suni Lee* is on file at the Library of Congress.
ISBN 978-1-7284-6383-4 (lib. bdg.)
ISBN 978-1-7284-6384-1 (pbk.)
ISBN 978-1-7284-6385-8 (eb pdf)

Manufactured in the United States of America
1-51615-50386-9/28/2021

TABLE OF CONTENTS

GOLD

Suni Lee performs a floor exercise at the Tokyo Olympics in 2021.

US gymnast Suni Lee sprinted across the padded floor. She raised her arms, flipped, and launched herself into the air. She twisted and turned before landing on her feet. Her vault score of 14.600 put her in fourth place.

- **Date of birth:** March 9, 2003

- **Position:** gymnast

- **League:** USA Gymnastics

- **Professional highlights:** became a junior member of the US Women's Artistic Gymnastics National Team at 14; finished second at the 2021 US Olympic Trials; won gold, silver, and bronze medals at the 2021 Olympic Games

- **Personal highlights:** grew up in St. Paul, Minnesota; practiced gymnastics in her backyard; began attending Auburn University in 2021

Lee was competing in the individual all-around at the Olympic Games in Tokyo, Japan. During the contest in July 2021, gymnasts performed in four different events. Judges combined the scores from each event to decide a winner.

On the uneven bars, Lee spun from one bar to the other. The event was often her best. Lee's 15.300 was the highest uneven bars score.

Lee on the uneven bars at the 2021 Olympics

At important competitions like the Olympics, the balance beam is a test of nerves. The beam is about 16 feet (4.8 m) long and just 4 inches (10 cm) wide. One wrong step can lead to disaster. But Lee's controlled leaps and flips earned a 13.833.

Lee was in first place. But her lead was only two-tenths of a point. The floor exercise was the final event. Lee's fun and difficult routine earned 13.700 points. The score was enough to win the all-around gold medal! "I didn't even think I'd ever get here," Lee said. "It doesn't even feel like I'm in real life."

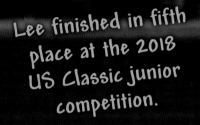

Lee finished in fifth place at the 2018 US Classic junior competition.

Sunisa Lee was born in St. Paul, Minnesota, on March 9, 2003. She has two sisters, Shyenne and Evionn. She also has three brothers: Lucky, Noah, and Jonah.

Left to right: Suni with her father, Lucky, and Evionn

Suni loved gymnastics from an early age, and she practiced at home. She learned to do flips by jumping on a bed. She even practiced flipping in her backyard on a wooden balance beam that her father, John, made.

When Suni was six years old, she began working with gymnastics coaches. Alison Lim and her husband, Jess Graba, run Midwest Gymnastics in Little Canada, Minnesota. They saw a lot of talent in Suni. They were impressed with her ability to jump and flip without fear.

Suni worked hard and kept improving. At 14, she became a junior member of the US Women's Artistic Gymnastics National Team. She began traveling around the world with the team to compete against gymnasts from other countries.

Lee's favorite movies are Finding Nemo and Just Go with It. She also loves the Harry Potter book series.

Suni keeps her eyes on the balance beam as she performs a flip.

In 2019, Suni was preparing to compete in the US Gymnastics Championships. Two days before the contest, her father was trimming trees. He fell off his ladder and injured his back and ribs. He could no longer move his body below his chest.

Her father's accident upset Suni. But her family encouraged her to focus on her sport. Watching on TV from his hospital bed, John saw Suni win a silver medal. "She can stay focused when she puts her mind to it," he said.

Two years later, Lee was ready to try out for the world's biggest gymnastics contest. In June 2021, she competed at the US Olympic Team Trials in St. Louis, Missouri. She finished in second place in the all-around behind superstar Simone Biles. Lee was going to Tokyo!

Lee (*second from left*) poses with the rest of Team USA after the 2021 US Olympic Team Trials.

WORLD-CLASS EFFORT

Lee stays focused while practicing the floor exercise.

Becoming an Olympic gymnast takes years of effort. Athletes work out to make their bodies agile and strong. They also spend thousands of hours practicing their routines.

Lee works out during practice at Midwest Gymnastics.

Gymnasts usually work out at least six days each week. They train twice a day to get ready for big contests like the Olympics. In the morning, they run, lift weights, and do other exercises to strengthen their bodies. Then they practice their routines and skills. In the afternoon, they do more strength training and practice other routines.

To be a world-class gymnast, Lee spends almost 40 hours each week working out and practicing. Spending all that time in the gym has made her close to her coaches. "My wife and I basically spend so much time with her that she's kind of like one of our kids," Graba said.

Lee poses with Graba at the 2021 Olympics. Graba began coaching Lee when she was six.

Lee gets a pep talk from her father before every competition. When she was a kid, he reminded her to stay focused. These days, he just tells her to have fun.

Lee's training schedule was disrupted in March 2020. The disease COVID-19 was spreading around the world. Like many businesses, Midwest Gymnastics shut down to avoid spreading the disease. For the first time in years, Lee couldn't spend time at the gym.

Midwest Gymnastics reopened in June. But just two weeks after returning to training, Lee fell from the uneven bars and twisted her ankle. She broke a bone in her foot and had to stop training again. While Lee was recovering, her aunt and uncle died. She leaned on her family for support, especially her sister Shyenne.

Lee returned to the gym that winter. She was back to full strength when she competed in the US Olympic Trials in June 2021. Her father watched her compete in person for the first time since his accident.

Lee had overcome a lot to earn her ticket to the Olympics. She was ready to compete and happy to represent her country. "It's been a tough year, but I'm super proud of myself," Lee said.

Lee's performance during the 2021 US Olympic Team Trials helped her make it to Tokyo.

Lee waves to the crowd during a celebration in St. Paul after the 2021 Olympics.

Lee takes a photo with a young fan after returning home from Tokyo.

Lee is the first Hmong American to represent the US in the Olympic Games.

Millions of Hmong people live in Southeast Asia. After the Vietnam War (1955–1975), many Hmong people moved to the US.

St. Paul, Minnesota

The St. Paul and Minneapolis, Minnesota, metro area has the largest Hmong community in the US. Lee's friends and family have supported her throughout her career, and she knows they're proud of her. She hopes to inspire young people in the Hmong community to reach for their dreams.

The St. Paul and Minneapolis Hmong community cheered for Lee during the Olympics. Her family arranged a party in Oakdale, Minnesota, to watch her compete. They planned for up to 100 people to attend. Instead, more than 300 people showed up to support Lee. They cheered and hugged one another when she won the gold medal.

Lee's family and friends celebrate as Lee wins Olympic gold.

After her final Olympics event, Lee traveled back to the United States. On August 4, she reunited with Shyenne in New York City. But she didn't get to see her parents until the next day. On August 5, Lee appeared on *Today* and saw her mother, father, Jonah, and Shyenne. She went straight to John and gave him a long and tearful hug.

After winning gold, Lee received messages from famous people to say they were proud and happy for her. Actors Brenda Song, Kerry Washington, and Reese Witherspoon all posted messages about Lee on social media.

On August 8, 2021, more than 20,000 people gathered along White Bear Avenue in St. Paul. They had come from all around the country to honor Lee. Minnesota governor Tim Walz, author Kao Kalia Yang, and many others watched Lee ride down the street on a fire truck. Alongside her mother and Shyenne, Lee waved to the crowd and showed off her gold medal.

After the parade, Lee spoke to the crowd. She thanked her family and community for their support. She said, "I'm so overwhelmed, and I really feel all of the love and support that all of you have given me throughout my whole entire journey and especially now since—I'm an Olympic gold medalist!"

Lee waves from a fire truck during the parade in 2021.

Before the individual all-around, Lee competed in the team all-around at the Tokyo Olympics. Lee and her teammates performed well. Team USA finished in second place and took home silver medals.

Lee's balance beam routine helped Team USA win silver at the 2021 Olympics.

Lee launches from the springboard to the vaulting table during the individual all-around at the 2021 Olympics.

The individual all-around was next. Lee beat Rebeca Andrade to win gold. Lee became the fifth US athlete in a row to win the Olympic all-around.

With two medals in her pocket, Lee turned to the event finals. She earned a bronze medal on uneven bars. She also competed on balance beam but didn't win a medal.

After the event finals, a reporter asked Lee what she planned to do next. "I don't even know," she said. "I'm going to go eat a pizza. That's all I've been craving this whole time."

Later that day, Lee posted a video on TikTok that showed her dancing with her gold medal and eating pizza.

Lee poses for photos after the individual all-around medal ceremony.

Lee returned to the US to celebrate with her friends and family. She had become an Olympic hero and one of the most famous athletes in the US. A few days later, she moved to Alabama to attend Auburn University and continue her gymnastics career. Fans can't wait to see her defend her gold medal at the next Olympics.

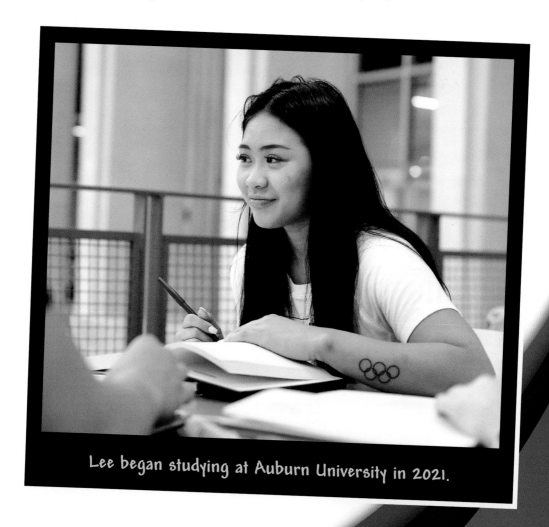

Lee began studying at Auburn University in 2021.

All-Star Stats

Gymnastics contests are often very close. One mistake can mean the difference between winning gold and not winning a medal. Take a look at the top 10 overall scores in the women's individual all-around at the Tokyo Olympics:

Gymnast	Country	Score
1. Suni Lee	United States	57.433
2. Rebeca Andrade	Brazil	57.298
3. Angelina Melnikova	Russian Olympic Committee	57.199
4. Vladislava Urazova	Russian Olympic Committee	56.966
5. Mai Murakami	Japan	56.032
6. Nina Derwael	Belgium	55.965
7. Tang Xijing	China	54.498
8. Jade Carey	United States	54.199
9. Elisabeth Seitz	Germany	54.066
10. Jessica Gadirova	Great Britain	53.965

Glossary

agile: able to move quickly and easily

balance beam: an event in which gymnasts perform on a 4-inch-wide (10 cm) beam

event: one of the contests in a sports competition

event finals: contests in which female athletes compete to decide the top gymnast on vault, uneven bars, balance beam, and floor exercise

floor exercise: an event in which gymnasts perform dance steps and tumbling moves on a 40-square-foot (3.7 sq. m) mat

individual all-around: when an athlete competes in all the events and is given a score in each

routine: the series of skills and artistic moves that gymnasts perform

team all-around: when athletes compete as teams in all the events and teammates' scores are combined

tryout: a test of the ability of an athlete to become a member of a team

uneven bars: an event in which gymnasts use two bars at different heights

vault: an event in which gymnasts launch from a springboard to a vaulting table and then into the air

Source Notes

7 Juliet Macur, "Olympic Gymnastics Updates: Sunisa Lee Wins All-Around Gold," *New York Times*, updated August 8, 2021, https://www.nytimes.com/live/2021/07/29/sports/gymnastics-olympics.

11 Rose Minutaglio and Madison Feller, "You Can't Stop Suni Lee," *Elle*, July 29, 2021, https://www.elle.com/culture/a36503849/suni-lee-olympics-gymnastics-tokyo/.

15 Melissa Goldberg, "U.S. Olympic Gymnast Sunisa Lee Continues Winning Streak with a Bronze on the Uneven Bars," *Oprah Daily*, August 2, 2021, https://www.oprahdaily.com/entertainment/a37115083/who-is-sunisa-lee/.

17 Alyssa Roenigk, "U.S. Gymnastics Star Sunisa Lee's Long, Winding Journey to Olympics 2021," *ESPN*, July 29, 2021, https://www.espn.com/olympics/story/_/id/31849287/us-gymnastics-star-sunisa-lee-long-winding-journey-olympics-2021.

23 "Crowds Line St. Paul Parade Route to Honor and Celebrate Olympic Champion Suni Lee," MPR News, August 8, 2021, https://www.mprnews.org/story/2021/08/08/crowds-line-st-paul-parade-route-to-honor-and-celebrate-olympic-champion-suni-lee.

26 Lisa Curran Matte, "Olympic Gymnast Sunisa Lee Ate This Food to Celebrate Her Gold Medal," *Mashed*, July 30, 2021, https://www.mashed.com/474970/olympic-gymnast-sunisa-lee-ate-this-food-to-celebrate-her-gold-medal/.

Learn More

Hmong in Minnesota—Minnesota Historical Society
https://www.mnhs.org/hmong

Levit, Joe. *Gymnastics's G.O.A.T.: Nadia Comaneci, Simone Biles, and More*. Minneapolis: Lerner Publications, 2022.

Nicks, Erin. *A Guide to Competitive Gymnastics*. Minneapolis: Abdo, 2021.

Scheff, Matt. *The Summer Olympics: World's Best Athletic Competition*. Minneapolis: Lerner Publications, 2021.

Sunisa Lee—Team USA
https://www.teamusa.org/usa-gymnastics/athletes/Sunisa-Lee

USA Gymnastics
https://usagym.org/

Index

Photo Acknowledgments

Image credits: Naoki Morita/AFLO/Shutterstock.com, p. 4; Jean Catuffe/Getty Images, p. 6; Joe Robbins/Getty Images, p. 8; Evan Frost/Minnesota Public Radio via AP, p. 9; Melissa J. Perenson/Cal Sport Media via AP Images, p. 11; Jamie Squire/Getty Images, pp. 12, 15, 26; Christine T. Nguyen/Minnesota Public Radio via AP, pp. 13, 14; Carmen Mandato/Getty Images, p. 17; John Autey/MediaNews Group/St. Paul Pioneer Press via Getty Images, p. 18; Glen Stubbe/Star Tribune via AP, p. 19; Paul Brady Photography/Shutterstock.com, p. 20; Stephen Maturen/Getty Images, p. 21; Nikolas Liepins/Shutterstock, p. 23; Chris Cooper/Action Plus/Shutterstock, p. 24; Morry Gash/AP/Shutterstock.com, p. 25; Shanna Lockwood/AU Athletics, p. 27.

Cover: DPPI/Kanami Yoshimura/LiveMedia/Shutterstock.com.